Mastering the IELTS Reading Section

Tips, Techniques, and Practice for Success

By Kirtish Datwani

Structure of the Book

This book is designed to provide comprehensive guidance on mastering the IELTS Reading section. It is structured to address the common challenges faced by test-takers and to offer practical tips, techniques, and practice materials to enhance reading skills. The chapters are organized as follows:

1. **Introduction**
   - Overview of the IELTS Reading Section
   - Importance of Reading Skills
2. **Understanding the IELTS Reading Section**
   - Types of Questions
   - Common Challenges
   - Scoring and Evaluation Criteria
3. **Reading Strategies and Techniques**
   - Skimming and Scanning
   - Detailed Reading
   - Identifying Keywords
   - Inferring Meaning from Context
   - Time Management
4. **Building Vocabulary**
   - Importance of Vocabulary in IELTS
   - Techniques for Vocabulary Building
   - Common IELTS Vocabulary Lists
   - Exercises and Flashcards
5. **Practice Passages and Questions**
   - Passage 1: Easy Level
     - Questions and Detailed Answer Explanations
   - Passage 2: Medium Level
     - Questions and Detailed Answer Explanations
   - Passage 3: Difficult Level
     - Questions and Detailed Answer Explanations
6. **Specialized Practice Sections**
   - True/False/Not Given Questions
   - Matching Headings to Paragraphs
   - Multiple Choice Questions
   - Summary Completion

7. **Mock Tests**
o   Full-Length Practice Tests
o   Answer Keys and Explanations

8. **Common Pitfalls and How to Avoid Them**
o   Misunderstanding the Question
o   Failing to Manage Time
o   Overlooking Keywords
o   Misinterpreting Information

9. **Tips from Successful Candidates**
o   Interviews and Insights
o   Personal Experiences and Strategies

10. **Additional Resources**
o   Recommended Books, Websites, and Apps
o   Further Reading Materials

By the end of this book, you will have a thorough understanding of the IELTS Reading section, along with practical strategies and ample practice materials to boost your confidence and improve your performance.

Chapter 1: Introduction

Title: Mastering the IELTS Reading Section: Tips and Techniques for Success

1.1 Overview of the IELTS Reading Section

The International English Language Testing System (IELTS) is a standardized test designed to assess the language proficiency of non-native English speakers. It is widely accepted by educational institutions, employers, and immigration authorities around the world. The IELTS test consists of four sections: Listening, Reading, Writing, and Speaking.

The Reading section is designed to evaluate a candidate's ability to understand and interpret written English. It comprises 40 questions that need to be answered within 60 minutes. The texts in the Reading section are taken from books, magazines, newspapers, and online resources, covering a wide range of topics, including social sciences, natural sciences, and everyday issues.

1.2 Importance of Reading Skills

Reading is a fundamental skill that plays a crucial role in academic and professional success. In the context of the IELTS exam, strong reading skills are essential for achieving a high band score. The ability to quickly comprehend and analyze written texts is not only important for the Reading section but also beneficial for the Writing and Speaking sections, where understanding prompts and context is vital.

Effective reading skills enable candidates to:

- Extract relevant information quickly.
- Understand complex ideas and arguments.
- Identify the main points and supporting details.
- Infer meanings and draw conclusions from the text.

Chapter 2: Understanding the IELTS Reading Section

2.1 Types of Questions

The IELTS Reading section includes a variety of question types designed to test different reading skills. Understanding these question types is essential for effective preparation. Here are the main types of questions you will encounter:

1. **Multiple Choice Questions (MCQs)**
   o **Description:** Select the correct answer from a list of options.
   o **Skills Tested:** Detailed understanding of specific points or overall comprehension of the main ideas.
2. **Identifying Information (True/False/Not Given)**
   o **Description:** Determine whether the statements are true, false, or not given based on the text.
   o **Skills Tested:** Ability to distinguish between factual information and opinions, and to identify explicitly stated information.
3. **Identifying the Writer's Views/Claims (Yes/No/Not Given)**
   o **Description:** Identify whether the writer's views or claims match the statements.
   o **Skills Tested:** Understanding of the writer's attitude, opinion, or purpose.
4. **Matching Information**
   o **Description:** Match information or statements to the correct part of the text.
   o **Skills Tested:** Locating specific information within the text and understanding detailed or general information.
5. **Matching Headings**
   o **Description:** Match headings to the appropriate paragraphs or sections of the text.
   o **Skills Tested:** Understanding the main idea of each paragraph or section.
6. **Matching Features**
   o **Description:** Match a list of features to the corresponding part of the text.
   o **Skills Tested:** Identifying relationships and connections between different pieces of information.
7. **Matching Sentence Endings**
   o **Description:** Complete sentences by matching the beginning of the sentence with the correct ending.
   o **Skills Tested:** Understanding how ideas or pieces of information are connected.

8. **Sentence Completion**
o **Description:** Complete sentences with a word or short phrase from the text.
o **Skills Tested:** Detailed understanding of specific points or overall comprehension.
9. **Summary, Note, Table, Flow-Chart Completion**
o **Description:** Complete summaries, notes, tables, or flow-charts using words from the text.
o **Skills Tested:** Ability to identify and understand key information.
10. **Diagram Label Completion**
o **Description:** Label a diagram with words from the text.
o **Skills Tested:** Understanding of detailed descriptions and ability to translate this information into a diagram.
11. **Short-Answer Questions**
o **Description:** Answer questions using words from the text.
o **Skills Tested:** Detailed understanding of specific points or overall comprehension.

2.2 Common Challenges

Many candidates face specific challenges when preparing for the IELTS Reading section. Here are some of the most common issues and how to address them:

1. **Time Management**
o **Challenge:** Running out of time before completing all questions.
o **Solution:** Practice under timed conditions and develop a strategy for allocating time to each section.
2. **Understanding Complex Texts**
o **Challenge:** Difficulty in understanding complex or technical texts.
o **Solution:** Regular reading of diverse materials to become familiar with different styles and vocabularies.
3. **Identifying Keywords**
o **Challenge:** Struggling to identify and use keywords effectively.
o **Solution:** Practice identifying keywords in questions and finding corresponding information in the text.
4. **Distinguishing True/False/Not Given and Yes/No/Not Given**
o **Challenge:** Confusion between what is explicitly stated and what is inferred or not mentioned.
o **Solution:** Careful reading and practice with distinguishing between these types of questions.

5. **Handling Unfamiliar Topics**
   - o **Challenge:** Difficulty in understanding and answering questions on unfamiliar topics.
   - o **Solution:** Broaden your reading to include a variety of subjects to build confidence and familiarity.

6. **Misinterpretation of Questions**
   - o **Challenge:** Misunderstanding what the question is asking.
   - o **Solution:** Pay close attention to the wording of the questions and practice paraphrasing them to ensure understanding.

2.3 Scoring and Evaluation Criteria

Understanding how the IELTS Reading section is scored can help you target your preparation more effectively. Here's an overview of the scoring system and what the examiners look for:

1. **Scoring System**
   - o Each correct answer is awarded one mark.
   - o There are 40 questions in total, and the raw score out of 40 is converted to the IELTS 9-band scale.
2. **Band Descriptors**
   - o The band descriptors provide detailed information about the level of performance required for each band score (e.g., Band 7, Band 8).
   - o Focus on the criteria for higher band scores to understand what is required to achieve them.
3. **Conversion Table**
   - o Familiarize yourself with the conversion table that translates raw scores into band scores.
   - o Example:
     - 39-40 = Band 9
     - 37-38 = Band 8.5
     - 35-36 = Band 8
     - 33-34 = Band 7.5

By understanding the types of questions, common challenges, and scoring criteria, you can approach the IELTS Reading section with greater confidence and a clear strategy.

Conversion Table for IELTS Reading Section

Raw Score Band Score

Raw Score	Band Score
39-40	9.0
37-38	8.5
35-36	8.0
33-34	7.5
30-32	7.0
27-29	6.5
23-26	6.0

This table provides a clear guideline for how your raw score on the reading section translates into the IELTS band scores. Use this table to set your target scores and track your progress during practice sessions.

Chapter 3: Reading Strategies and Techniques

3.1 Skimming and Scanning

Effective reading strategies are essential for success in the IELTS Reading section. Two key techniques are skimming and scanning.

Skimming

- **Definition:** Quickly reading through a text to get a general idea of the content.
- **Purpose:** To understand the main ideas and structure of the passage.
- **Technique:**
  o Read the title and headings.
  o Look at any subheadings, illustrations, and captions.
  o Read the first and last sentences of each paragraph.
  o Quickly go through the rest of the text to pick up key words and phrases.

Scanning

- **Definition:** Looking through a text quickly to find specific information.
- **Purpose:** To locate answers to specific questions.
- **Technique:**
  o Identify the keywords in the question.
  o Run your eyes over the text looking for these keywords or synonyms.
  o Once found, read the surrounding text more carefully to find the answer.

Practice Exercise:

Passage Excerpt:

"The Great Barrier Reef, located off the coast of Queensland, Australia, is the world's largest coral reef system. It is composed of over 2,900 individual reefs and 900 islands stretching for over 2,300 kilometers. The reef is home to a diverse range of marine life, including over 1,500 species of fish, 411 types of hard coral, and dozens of species of birds and mammals."

Questions:

1. What is the Great Barrier Reef composed of?
2. How many species of fish are found in the Great Barrier Reef?

Answers:

1. Over 2,900 individual reefs and 900 islands.
2. Over 1,500 species of fish.

3.2 Detailed Reading

Detailed Reading

- **Definition:** Reading thoroughly to understand detailed information and grasp the finer points.
- **Purpose:** To answer questions that require in-depth comprehension.
- **Technique:**
  o Read the passage carefully and note important details.
  o Pay attention to connectors and transitions.
  o Take notes or underline key points if necessary.

Practice Exercise:

Passage Excerpt:

"The Amazon Rainforest, often referred to as the lungs of the planet, plays a crucial role in regulating the Earth's climate. It produces approximately 20% of the world's oxygen and absorbs large amounts of carbon dioxide. Deforestation, however, poses a significant threat to this vital ecosystem. Each year, vast areas of the forest are cleared for agriculture, logging, and other purposes, leading to loss of biodiversity and disruption of the global climate."

Questions:

1. What percentage of the world's oxygen is produced by the Amazon Rainforest?
2. What are the main causes of deforestation in the Amazon Rainforest?

Answers:

1. Approximately 20%.
2. Agriculture, logging, and other purposes.

3.3 Identifying Keywords

Identifying Keywords

- **Definition:** Recognizing important words in a question that help locate the relevant part of the text.
- **Purpose:** To efficiently find the information needed to answer questions.
- **Technique:**
  - Highlight or underline keywords in the question.
  - Look for synonyms and paraphrased versions of these keywords in the text.
  - Use keywords to guide your skimming and scanning efforts.

Practice Exercise:

Question: "What are the main threats to the Amazon Rainforest?"

Keywords: Main threats, Amazon Rainforest.

Text: "Deforestation, however, poses a significant threat to this vital ecosystem. Each year, vast areas of the forest are cleared for agriculture, logging, and other purposes, leading to loss of biodiversity and disruption of the global climate."

3.4 Inferring Meaning from Context

Inferring Meaning

- **Definition:** Understanding the meaning of a word or phrase based on the context in which it appears.
- **Purpose:** To grasp the full meaning of the text even when unfamiliar words are encountered.
- **Technique:**
  - Look at the surrounding words and sentences.
  - Consider the overall context and topic.
  - Use knowledge of word roots, prefixes, and suffixes.

Practice Exercise:

Sentence: "The rapid deforestation of the Amazon is exacerbating the problem of climate change."

Question: What does "exacerbating" mean?

Context Clues: The sentence indicates that deforestation is making the problem of climate change worse.

Answer: Making worse.

3.5 Time Management

Time Management

- **Importance:** Effective time management ensures that you can answer all questions within the allotted 60 minutes.
- **Strategies:**
  o Allocate time based on the number of questions and difficulty of the passage.
  o Don't spend too much time on any one question.
  o Move on and come back to difficult questions if time permits.
  o Practice with a timer to get a sense of the pace needed.

Practice Exercise:

Timed Reading Passage:

Passage Excerpt:

"The Industrial Revolution was a period of profound change that transformed agriculture, manufacturing, and transportation. It began in Britain in the late 18th century and spread to other parts of the world. The introduction of machinery, such as the steam engine, played a significant role in increasing production and efficiency. However, it also led to significant social changes, including urbanization and the rise of factory-based labor."

Questions:

1. Where did the Industrial Revolution begin?
2. What was one major consequence of the Industrial Revolution?

Answers:

1. Britain.
2. Urbanization and the rise of factory-based labor.

By mastering these reading strategies and techniques, you will be better equipped to tackle the IELTS Reading section effectively and efficiently.

Chapter 4: Building Vocabulary

4.1 Importance of Vocabulary in IELTS

A strong vocabulary is crucial for success in the IELTS Reading section. It enables you to understand the text more clearly and quickly, infer the meaning of unknown words from context, and answer questions accurately.

Key Benefits of a Strong Vocabulary:

- **Comprehension:** Understanding complex texts becomes easier.
- **Speed:** Reading speed increases as you recognize more words.
- **Accuracy:** You can infer the meanings of unknown words and understand subtle differences in meaning.

4.2 Techniques for Vocabulary Building

Building a robust vocabulary takes time and consistent effort. Here are some effective techniques:

1. **Reading Widely and Regularly**
   - Read books, newspapers, journals, and online articles on various topics.
   - Exposure to different subjects helps you learn new words in context.
2. **Using a Dictionary and Thesaurus**
   - Look up unfamiliar words and their meanings.
   - Use a thesaurus to find synonyms and antonyms, which can expand your vocabulary.
3. **Making Vocabulary Lists**
   - Keep a notebook or digital document of new words.
   - Include definitions, example sentences, and any synonyms or antonyms.
4. **Flashcards**
   - Create flashcards with the word on one side and the definition on the other.
   - Review them regularly to reinforce your memory.
5. **Word Games and Apps**

- Use apps and games designed to improve vocabulary, such as crossword puzzles, word search games, and vocabulary-building apps.

6. **Practice Using New Words**

- Incorporate new words into your writing and speaking.
- This helps reinforce your understanding and memory of the words.

4.3 Common IELTS Vocabulary Lists

Here are some common words and phrases that frequently appear in IELTS Reading passages. Familiarizing yourself with these can give you a head start.

Academic Words:

- Analyze
- Approach
- Assess
- Assume
- Concept
- Consistent
- Derive
- Establish
- Estimate
- Evident
- Identify
- Indicate
- Interpret
- Involve
- Occur

Descriptive Words:

- Abundant
- Adequate
- Beneficial
- Complex
- Diverse
- Effective
- Extensive
- Fundamental

- Significant
- Substantial
- Unprecedented
- Widespread

Transition Words:

- Additionally
- Consequently
- Furthermore
- Hence
- However
- Moreover
- Nevertheless
- On the other hand
- Therefore
- Thus

Topic-Specific Words:

- Environment: Ecosystem, biodiversity, conservation, sustainable
- Technology: Innovation, digital, cybersecurity, automation
- Health: Wellness, nutrition, diagnosis, treatment

4.4 Exercises and Flashcards

Vocabulary List Exercise:

Create a list of new vocabulary words from a recent article you read. For each word, write the definition and use it in a sentence.

Example:

- **Word:** Sustainable
- **Definition:** Capable of being maintained over the long term without harming the environment.
- **Sentence:** The company adopted sustainable practices to reduce its environmental footprint.

Flashcard Exercise:

Create flashcards using the following words:

- **Analyze**
- **Beneficial**
- **Consequently**
- **Ecosystem**
- **Innovation**

On one side, write the word. On the other side, write the definition and an example sentence. Review these flashcards daily.

Word Association Exercise:

Group the following words into categories (e.g., academic, descriptive, transition):

- Effective
- Concept
- Nevertheless
- Adequate
- Consequently

Reading Comprehension Exercise:

Read a passage and underline all unfamiliar words. Look them up in a dictionary, write their definitions, and create example sentences.

Chapter 5: Practice Passages and Questions

In this chapter, we'll provide practice passages and questions to help you apply the techniques and strategies you've learned. Each passage will be accompanied by questions and detailed answer explanations.

5.1 Passage 1: Easy Level

Passage:

"The honeybee is a remarkable insect that plays a crucial role in pollinating many of the crops humans rely on for food. Honeybees live in colonies that can number in the tens of thousands. Each colony has a single queen bee, whose primary function is to lay eggs. Worker bees, which are all female, perform various tasks such as foraging for nectar, caring for the young, and maintaining the hive. Male bees, called drones, have the sole purpose of mating with the queen."

Questions:

1. What role does the queen bee play in the honeybee colony?
2. How many bees can be found in a honeybee colony?
3. What is the primary function of worker bees?
4. What is the sole purpose of drones in a honeybee colony?

Answers:

1. The queen bee's primary function is to lay eggs.
2. A honeybee colony can number in the tens of thousands.
3. Worker bees perform tasks such as foraging for nectar, caring for the young, and maintaining the hive.
4. The sole purpose of drones is to mate with the queen.

5.2 Passage 2: Medium Level

Passage:

"The Industrial Revolution, which began in the late 18th century, marked a significant turning point in history. It was characterized by the transition from agrarian economies to industrialized and urban societies. This period saw the invention of machinery that revolutionized manufacturing processes. The steam engine, invented by James Watt, played a pivotal role in this transformation. Factories began to emerge, and mass production became possible. However, the Industrial Revolution also brought about social changes, including urbanization and the rise of a working class. While it led to economic growth and technological advancements, it also resulted in harsh working conditions and environmental pollution."

Questions:

1. What was the Industrial Revolution characterized by?
2. Who invented the steam engine?
3. What were some of the social changes brought about by the Industrial Revolution?
4. What were some of the negative effects of the Industrial Revolution?

Answers:

1. The Industrial Revolution was characterized by the transition from agrarian economies to industrialized and urban societies.
2. James Watt invented the steam engine.
3. Some of the social changes included urbanization and the rise of a working class.
4. Negative effects included harsh working conditions and environmental pollution.

5.3 Passage 3: Difficult Level

Passage:

"Climate change is one of the most pressing issues facing the world today. It refers to significant changes in global temperatures and weather patterns over time. While climate change is a natural phenomenon, scientific evidence shows that human activities, particularly the burning of fossil fuels and deforestation, are accelerating the process. The consequences of climate change are far-reaching, affecting ecosystems, sea levels, and weather patterns. For instance, rising temperatures are causing polar ice caps to melt, leading to sea-level rise. Additionally, extreme weather events, such as hurricanes and

droughts, are becoming more frequent and severe. Addressing climate change requires global cooperation and significant changes in energy consumption and land use."

Questions:

1. What does climate change refer to?
2. What human activities are accelerating climate change?
3. What are some consequences of climate change mentioned in the passage?
4. Why is addressing climate change considered to require global cooperation?

Answers:

1. Climate change refers to significant changes in global temperatures and weather patterns over time.
2. Human activities such as the burning of fossil fuels and deforestation are accelerating climate change.
3. Some consequences include the melting of polar ice caps, sea-level rise, and more frequent and severe extreme weather events.
4. Addressing climate change is considered to require global cooperation because it affects the entire planet and significant changes in energy consumption and land use are needed.

Detailed Answer Explanations

Passage 1 Explanation:

1. The queen bee's primary function is to lay eggs. This is directly stated in the passage.
2. The passage states that a honeybee colony can number in the tens of thousands.
3. Worker bees perform various tasks such as foraging for nectar, caring for the young, and maintaining the hive, as mentioned in the passage.
4. The passage clearly states that the sole purpose of drones is to mate with the queen.

Passage 2 Explanation:

1. The passage describes the Industrial Revolution as the transition from agrarian economies to industrialized and urban societies.
2. The steam engine was invented by James Watt, as mentioned in the passage.
3. Social changes brought about by the Industrial Revolution include urbanization and the rise of a working class.
4. The passage mentions that the Industrial Revolution resulted in harsh working conditions and environmental pollution.

Passage 3 Explanation:

1. Climate change refers to significant changes in global temperatures and weather patterns over time, as defined in the passage.
2. The passage states that human activities, particularly the burning of fossil fuels and deforestation, are accelerating climate change.
3. Consequences of climate change mentioned in the passage include the melting of polar ice caps, sea-level rise, and more frequent and severe extreme weather events.
4. Addressing climate change requires global cooperation because it affects the entire planet and significant changes in energy consumption and land use are needed, as mentioned in the passage.

Chapter 6: Specialized Practice Sections

In this chapter, we will focus on specialized practice sections that simulate the different question types found in the IELTS Reading section. Each section will include practice passages followed by questions.

6.1 Multiple Choice Questions (MCQs)

Passage:

"Artificial intelligence (AI) is a rapidly advancing field with applications across various industries. AI systems are designed to perform tasks that typically require human intelligence, such as speech recognition, decision-making, and visual perception. One of the key challenges in AI development is ensuring that these systems are ethical and unbiased. As AI becomes more integrated into daily life, concerns about privacy, job displacement, and algorithmic fairness have emerged. Despite these challenges, AI has the potential to revolutionize healthcare, transportation, and education."

Questions:

1. According to the passage, what are AI systems designed to do?
   - A) Play chess and solve puzzles
   - B) Perform tasks that require human intelligence
   - C) Create artwork and music
   - D) None of the above
2. What is mentioned as a key challenge in AI development?
   - A) Speed and efficiency
   - B) Ethics and bias
   - C) Integration with social media
   - D) Academic research

Answers:

1. B) Perform tasks that require human intelligence.
2. B) Ethics and bias.

6.2 True/False/Not Given Questions

Passage:

"The Internet of Things (IoT) refers to the network of physical devices embedded with sensors, software, and connectivity to exchange data. These devices range from everyday household items, such as smart speakers and thermostats, to industrial machinery and vehicles. The IoT allows for automation and remote control, improving efficiency and convenience. However, concerns about data security and privacy have arisen as the number of connected devices continues to grow."

Questions:

1. The IoT includes only industrial machinery and vehicles.
- o True
- o False
- o Not Given
2. Privacy concerns have not been raised about the IoT.
- o True
- o False
- o Not Given

Answers:

1. False (The IoT includes everyday household items as well.)
2. Not Given (Privacy concerns are mentioned, but it is not stated whether they have been completely raised or not.)

6.3 Matching Headings Questions

Passage:

"Globalization is the process of increased interconnectedness among countries, economies, and cultures. It has been driven by advancements in technology, communication, and transportation. Globalization has led to the expansion of international trade, cultural exchange, and migration. Critics argue that globalization has widened economic inequalities and threatened local cultures. Supporters believe it promotes economic growth and cultural diversity."

Paragraphs:

1. Globalization is the process of increased interconnectedness among countries, economies, and cultures. It has been driven by advancements in technology, communication, and transportation.
2. Globalization has led to the expansion of international trade, cultural exchange, and migration.
3. Critics argue that globalization has widened economic inequalities and threatened local cultures.
4. Supporters believe it promotes economic growth and cultural diversity.

Headings:

A) Advantages of globalization

B) Criticisms of globalization

C) Definition of globalization

Questions:

Match each heading to the corresponding paragraph in the passage.

Answers:

- A) Advantages of globalization: Paragraph 4
- B) Criticisms of globalization: Paragraph 3
- C) Definition of globalization: Paragraph 1

Detailed Answer Explanations

Each question type in this chapter is designed to mimic the format and complexity of questions found in the IELTS Reading section. Review the answers and explanations to understand how to approach each type effectively.

Chapter 7: Full-Length Practice Test

In this chapter, we will provide a full-length practice test designed to simulate the conditions of the IELTS Reading section. Each passage will cover a variety of question types commonly found in the actual exam.

Instructions:

- Set a timer for 60 minutes to simulate the actual exam conditions.
- Answer all questions based on the passages provided.
- Follow the specific instructions for each question type carefully.

Passage 1: The History and Impact of Photography

Photography, the art and science of capturing images, has a history that dates back to the early 19th century. The invention of photography revolutionized the way people view and understand the world, providing a new medium for capturing and preserving moments in time.

The earliest form of photography, known as the daguerreotype, was developed by Louis Daguerre in 1839. This process involved exposing a silver-plated copper sheet to iodine vapor to create a light-sensitive surface. The plate was then exposed to light in a camera, developed with mercury vapor, and fixed with a salt solution. Despite its complexity, the daguerreotype quickly gained popularity due to its ability to produce highly detailed images.

Over the next few decades, numerous advancements were made in photographic technology. The invention of the calotype process by William Henry Fox Talbot in 1841 introduced the concept of negative and positive images, allowing for multiple prints from a single exposure. This was a significant improvement over the daguerreotype, which produced only one-of-a-kind images.

In the late 19th and early 20th centuries, the development of roll film by George Eastman and the introduction of the Kodak camera made photography more accessible to the general public. The Kodak camera was simple to use and came pre-loaded with a roll of film, allowing users to take multiple photographs before sending the camera back to the company for processing.

The impact of photography on society has been profound. It has transformed journalism, art, and science, providing new ways to document and communicate information. In journalism, photographs have the power to convey stories and emotions more effectively than words alone.

In art, photography has opened up new avenues for creative expression, challenging traditional notions of what constitutes art. In science, photographs have become essential tools for research and documentation, from capturing microscopic details to documenting celestial events.

Despite its many benefits, photography has also raised ethical and legal concerns. Issues such as privacy, consent, and manipulation of images have sparked debates about the responsibilities of photographers and the potential misuse of photographic technology. The digital age has further complicated these issues, as the ease of sharing and altering images has made it more difficult to ensure the authenticity and integrity of photographs.

Today, photography continues to evolve with advancements in digital technology. High-resolution cameras, smartphone photography, and image editing software have made it easier than ever to capture and share images. As technology continues to advance, the future of photography promises to bring even more exciting developments and possibilities.

Questions 1-6

Answer the following questions using NO MORE THAN TWO WORDS for each answer.

1. What was the earliest form of photography mentioned in the passage?
2. Who developed the calotype process?
3. How did the Kodak camera change photography for the general public?
4. What are some ways photography has impacted journalism?
5. What ethical concerns are associated with photography?
6. How has digital technology affected photography?

Questions 7-12

Do the following statements agree with the information given in the passage? Write:

- **TRUE** if the statement agrees with the information
- **FALSE** if the statement contradicts the information
- **NOT GIVEN** if there is no information on this

7. The daguerreotype process was simple and easy to use.
8. The calotype process allowed for the production of multiple prints from a single exposure.
9. The Kodak camera was introduced in the early 19th century.
10. Photography has transformed traditional notions of art.
11. Ethical concerns about photography only began in the digital age.
12. High-resolution cameras and smartphones have made it harder to share images.

Questions 13-15

Choose the correct heading for paragraphs from the list of headings below. Write the correct number i-vi next to the paragraphs 13-15.

List of Headings:

i) The Origins of Photography ii) The Evolution of Photographic Technology iii) The Impact of Photography on Society iv) Ethical and Legal Issues in Photography v) The Future of Photography

13. Paragraph 1 _____
14. Paragraph 2 _____
15. Paragraph 4 _____

Passage 2: Renewable Energy and Sustainable Development

Renewable energy sources, such as solar, wind, and hydroelectric power, are becoming increasingly important in the global effort to combat climate change and promote sustainable development. Unlike fossil fuels, which are finite and contribute to greenhouse gas emissions, renewable energy sources are abundant and environmentally friendly.

Solar energy, harnessed from the sun's rays, is one of the most promising sources of renewable energy. Advances in photovoltaic technology have made solar panels more efficient and affordable, leading to widespread adoption in both residential and commercial settings. Solar farms, which consist of large arrays of solar panels, have been established in many parts of the world to generate electricity on a large scale.

One of the key benefits of solar energy is its ability to provide power in remote and off-grid locations, improving energy access for communities that lack traditional infrastructure.

Wind energy, generated by converting wind currents into electricity using wind turbines, is another major source of renewable energy. Wind farms, often located in rural or coastal areas, can produce significant amounts of electricity with minimal environmental impact. The efficiency and capacity of wind turbines have improved dramatically in recent years, making wind energy one of the fastest-growing renewable energy sectors. However, challenges such as noise pollution, impact on wildlife, and aesthetic concerns continue to be addressed.

Hydroelectric power, produced by harnessing the energy of flowing or falling water, has been a reliable source of renewable energy for over a century. Large-scale hydroelectric dams, such as the Hoover Dam in the United States and the Three Gorges Dam in China, generate substantial amounts of electricity and provide water for irrigation and flood control. In addition to large dams, small-scale hydroelectric systems, known as micro-hydro projects, are being implemented in rural areas to support local energy needs.

The transition to renewable energy is essential for achieving sustainable development goals. By reducing dependence on fossil fuels, renewable energy sources help mitigate climate change, reduce air pollution, and promote energy security. Additionally, the renewable energy sector creates jobs and stimulates economic growth, contributing to poverty alleviation and social development.

Despite these benefits, the widespread adoption of renewable energy faces several challenges. High initial costs, technological barriers, and the need for supportive policies and infrastructure are significant obstacles. Additionally, integrating renewable energy into existing power grids requires careful planning and management to ensure reliability and stability.

International cooperation and investment are crucial for overcoming these challenges and accelerating the transition to renewable energy. Global initiatives, such as the Paris Agreement, aim to foster collaboration and commitment among nations to reduce greenhouse gas emissions and promote sustainable development. As renewable energy technologies continue to advance, they hold the potential to transform the global energy landscape and pave the way for a more sustainable future.

Questions 16-21

Answer the following questions using NO MORE THAN THREE WORDS for each answer.

16. What are some benefits of solar energy mentioned in the passage?
17. How has wind energy capacity improved in recent years?
18. What are some challenges associated with wind energy?
19. What roles do large-scale hydroelectric dams play?
20. How do micro-hydro projects support local energy needs?
21. What are some economic benefits of the renewable energy sector?

Questions 22-26

Do the following statements agree with the information given in the passage? Write:

- **TRUE** if the statement agrees with the information
- **FALSE** if the statement contradicts the information
- **NOT GIVEN** if there is no information on this

22. Solar energy can provide power in off-grid locations.
23. Wind energy is the slowest-growing renewable energy sector.
24. The Hoover Dam generates hydroelectric power and provides water for irrigation.
25. High initial costs are not a barrier to the adoption of renewable energy.
26. The Paris Agreement aims to reduce greenhouse gas emissions.

Questions 27-30

Complete the sentences below with words taken from the passage. Use NO MORE THAN THREE WORDS for each answer.

27. Renewable energy sources are _______ and environmentally friendly.
28. Solar farms have been established in many parts of the world to generate _______.
29. The efficiency and capacity of wind turbines have improved _______ in recent years.
30. Global initiatives like the Paris Agreement aim to foster _______ among nations.

Passage 3: The Psychology of Learning and Memory

Understanding the mechanisms behind learning and memory is crucial for developing effective educational strategies and enhancing cognitive performance. Research in cognitive psychology has identified several factors that influence how information is acquired, retained, and recalled.

Paragraph A One of the key principles in learning is the spacing effect, which suggests that information is more effectively encoded and retained when study sessions are spaced out over time. This means that students should aim to review material multiple times over a longer period, rather than cramming all at once. Spacing out learning helps improve long-term retention and makes it easier to recall information when needed.

Paragraph B Another critical factor in learning and memory is attention. Attention acts as a filter, determining which information is processed and encoded into memory. Strategies to enhance attention include minimizing distractions, focusing on one task at a time, and employing active learning techniques. Multitasking, often perceived as efficient, can actually impair learning and memory by dividing attention between multiple tasks.

Paragraph C Mnemonic devices are tools that aid in the encoding and retrieval of information. These techniques often involve associating new information with familiar concepts or creating vivid mental images. The method of loci, for example, involves associating information with specific locations, making it easier to remember sequences or lists.

Paragraph D Sleep plays a crucial role in memory consolidation, the process by which newly acquired information is stabilized and integrated into long-term memory. During sleep, the brain replays and reorganizes information, strengthening neural connections. Both the quantity and quality of sleep are important for optimal memory performance, highlighting the need for good sleep hygiene practices.

Paragraph E Emotion significantly influences learning and memory. Emotionally charged events are often remembered more vividly and accurately than neutral events, a phenomenon known as the emotional enhancement effect. This occurs because emotions activate the amygdala, a brain region involved in processing emotional information, which enhances the encoding and storage of memories.

Paragraph F The context in which learning occurs also impacts memory. The context-dependent memory effect suggests that information is more easily recalled when the context at retrieval matches the context at encoding. This principle can be applied by creating consistent study environments and using context cues to aid recall during exams or presentations.

Questions 31-35

Answer the following questions using NO MORE THAN THREE WORDS for each answer.

31. What strengthens memory through practice and repetition?
32. What determines which information is processed and encoded into memory?
33. What are mnemonic devices used for?
34. What process stabilizes and integrates new information into long-term memory?
35. What phenomenon causes emotionally charged events to be remembered more vividly?

Questions 36-40

Do the following statements agree with the information given in the passage? Write:

- **YES** if the statement agrees with the information
- **NO** if the statement contradicts the information
- **NOT GIVEN** if there is no information on this

36. Cramming is more effective than spaced practice for long-term memory retention.
37. Multitasking can improve learning outcomes.
38. The method of loci involves associating information with specific locations.
39. Sleep deprivation has no impact on memory processes.
40. Emotionally neutral events are remembered better than emotionally charged events.

Questions 41-43

Choose the correct heading for paragraphs from the list of headings below. Write the correct number i-vi next to the paragraphs 41-43.

List of Headings:

i) The Spacing Effect in Learning ii) Attention and Memory iii) Mnemonic Devices and Memory Techniques iv) The Role of Sleep in Memory Consolidation v) Emotional Influence on Memory vi) Context-Dependent Memory

41. Paragraph A _____
42. Paragraph B _____
43. Paragraph D _____

Answer Keys

Passage 1: The History and Impact of Photography

Questions 1-6:

1. daguerreotype
2. William Henry Fox Talbot
3. made photography more accessible
4. convey stories and emotions
5. privacy, consent
6. digital technology

Questions 7-12:

7. FALSE
8. TRUE
9. FALSE
10. TRUE
11. FALSE
12. FALSE

Questions 13-15:

13. i
14. ii
15. iv

Passage 2: Renewable Energy and Sustainable Development

Questions 16-21:

16. efficient, affordable, power in remote locations
17. improved dramatically
18. noise pollution, impact on wildlife, aesthetic concerns
19. generate electricity, provide water for irrigation and flood control
20. support local energy needs
21. creates jobs, stimulates economic growth

Questions 22-26:

22. TRUE
23. FALSE
24. TRUE
25. FALSE
26. TRUE

Questions 27-30:

27. abundant
28. electricity
29. dramatically
30. collaboration

Passage 3: The Psychology of Learning and Memory

Questions 31-35:

31. The spacing effect
32. Attention
33. encoding and retrieval
34. memory consolidation
35. emotional enhancement effect

Questions 36-40:

36. NO
37. NO
38. YES
39. NO
40. NO

Questions 41-43:

41. i
42. ii
43. iv

Chapter 8: Common Pitfalls in IELTS Reading and How to Avoid Them

In this chapter, we will explore common pitfalls that test-takers often encounter in the IELTS Reading section and provide strategies to overcome them effectively.

Common Pitfalls and How to Avoid Them

1. Misunderstanding the Question

Issue: Test-takers sometimes misinterpret the question requirements, leading to incorrect answers.

Solution: Follow these steps to avoid misunderstanding questions:

- **Read Carefully:** Pay close attention to the question wording and instructions.
- **Identify Key Elements:** Highlight keywords or phrases that indicate what the question is asking for.
- **Compare with Passage:** Double-check your answer against the passage to ensure it directly addresses the question.

2. Failing to Manage Time

Issue: Many candidates struggle with time management, either spending too long on certain questions or rushing through others.

Solution: Implement these strategies to manage your time effectively:

- **Allocate Time:** Divide your time among the passages based on their length. Aim for about 20 minutes per passage.
- **Prioritize Questions:** Start with easier questions to build momentum and save more challenging ones for later.
- **Practice Timed Tests:** Regularly practice under timed conditions to improve your pacing and decision-making under pressure.

3. Overlooking Keywords

Issue: Key information in the passages and questions can be missed if candidates overlook important keywords.

Solution: Develop techniques to identify and utilize keywords effectively:

- **Underline or Highlight:** Mark keywords in both the passage and the questions to help focus your attention.
- **Use Keywords in Answers:** Incorporate the same keywords from the passage into your answers where applicable.
- **Practice Keyword Identification:** Practice with sample questions to improve your ability to identify and utilize keywords.

4. Misinterpreting Information

Issue: Incorrectly interpreting information in the passage can lead to incorrect answers.

Solution: Improve your comprehension and interpretation skills with these methods:

- **Read Actively:** Engage with the text actively by summarizing each paragraph in your own words.
- **Verify Information:** Cross-check details and facts within the passage to ensure accurate understanding.
- **Practice Inference:** Practice drawing conclusions and making logical inferences based on the information provided.

Practice Exercise

Apply the strategies mentioned above to the following passage and questions:

Reading Passage

Paragraph A

As the world becomes more interconnected through globalization, the challenges faced by multinational corporations (MNCs) are increasingly complex. MNCs must navigate cultural differences, regulatory frameworks, and economic fluctuations across various markets. Understanding local consumer behavior and adapting strategies accordingly are crucial for their success.

Questions:

1. How can you avoid misinterpreting information in a passage?
2. What strategies should you use to manage your time effectively during the IELTS Reading section?
3. Why is it important to identify keywords in both the passage and the questions?
4. Describe a common pitfall related to misunderstanding the question in the IELTS Reading test.
5. How does active reading contribute to better comprehension in the IELTS Reading section?

Answers:

1. By reading carefully, identifying key elements in the question, and comparing answers with the passage.
2. By allocating time evenly across passages, prioritizing easier questions, and practicing timed tests.
3. Keywords help focus attention and ensure answers are aligned with information in the passage.
4. Misinterpreting question requirements can lead to incorrect answers despite understanding the passage.
5. Active reading promotes engagement with the text, aiding in better understanding and retention.

Conclusion

By recognizing and addressing these common pitfalls, you can significantly enhance your performance in the IELTS Reading section. Practice applying these strategies consistently to build confidence and improve your ability to navigate through the test effectively.

Chapter 9: Tips from Successful Candidates

In this chapter, we will draw insights from successful IELTS candidates, exploring their personal experiences, strategies, and valuable tips for excelling in the IELTS Reading section.

Interviews and Insights

Objective: Learn from the experiences and strategies of successful IELTS candidates to improve your own approach to the test.

Insights and Strategies:

- **Time Management:** Successful candidates emphasize the importance of allocating time effectively across passages and questions.
- **Critical Reading Skills:** Strategies for critical analysis of passages to extract key information and infer meaning.
- **Exam Preparation:** Insights into effective study routines, including practice tests and review of question types.
- **Stress Management:** Techniques for staying calm and focused during the exam to maintain clarity of thought.

Interview Excerpts:

Interviewee 1:

"I found that practicing with timed tests helped me improve my pacing and decision-making under pressure. It reduced my anxiety during the actual exam."

Interviewee 2:

"Understanding the structure of each passage was crucial. It allowed me to quickly locate information and answer questions accurately."

Personal Experiences and Strategies

Objective: Gain firsthand accounts of successful candidates' personal experiences and the strategies they employed to achieve their desired scores.

Strategies Shared:

- **Reading Techniques:** Approaches such as skimming for main ideas and scanning for specific details.
- **Vocabulary Development:** Methods for expanding academic and specialized vocabulary.
- **Feedback Utilization:** Importance of learning from mistakes and feedback provided during practice sessions.
- **Continuous Improvement:** Strategies for ongoing improvement through regular practice and review.

Personal Insights:

Candidate A:

"I dedicated specific time each day to study different question types. It helped me become more familiar with the format and improve my accuracy."

Candidate B:

"Taking practice tests under exam conditions was invaluable. It not only boosted my confidence but also highlighted areas where I needed more practice."

Conclusion

Learning from the experiences and strategies of successful candidates can provide valuable insights and inspiration for your own IELTS preparation journey. Incorporate these tips into your study routine to enhance your skills and confidence in the IELTS Reading section.

Chapter 10: Additional Resources for IELTS Preparation

In this chapter, we will explore valuable resources beyond this book that can further enhance your preparation for the IELTS Reading section.

Recommended Books, Websites, and Apps

Objective: Discover useful books, websites, and mobile applications that offer comprehensive study materials and practice resources for the IELTS exam.

1. Books:

- **"IELTS Official Practice Materials"** by Cambridge University Press: Offers authentic practice tests and helpful tips from the makers of the IELTS exam.
- **"The Official Cambridge Guide to IELTS"** by Pauline Cullen: Provides in-depth guidance and practice exercises for all sections of the IELTS exam.

2. Websites:

- **IELTS.org:** Official website offering sample questions, practice tests, and exam information.
- **British Council IELTS:** Provides tips, practice tests, and online resources for IELTS preparation.

3. Mobile Apps:

- **IELTS Prep App by British Council:** Offers interactive exercises, practice tests, and tips for IELTS preparation.
- **IELTS Practice & IELTS Test by Tutorials:** Provides mock tests, vocabulary exercises, and study tips.

Further Reading Materials

Objective: Explore additional reading materials that can broaden your understanding and knowledge base for the IELTS Reading section.

1. Academic Journals and Articles:

- **JSTOR:** Provides access to a wide range of academic articles across various disciplines.
- **Google Scholar:** Offers scholarly articles, theses, books, and conference papers.

2. English Language Newspapers and Magazines:

- **The Guardian:** Offers articles on current affairs, culture, and opinion pieces.
- **The Economist:** Provides articles on global news, business, finance, and economics.

Conclusion

Utilizing these additional resources alongside the strategies and techniques discussed in this book will enrich your preparation and improve your performance in the IELTS Reading section. Explore these options to tailor your study approach and achieve your desired score.

About the Author

Kirtish Datwani is a seasoned foreign education consultant with a passion for guiding students on their study abroad journeys. With over nine years of experience in the industry since 2015, he has successfully counseled more than 5000 students. Kirtish's expertise lies in helping aspiring students navigate the complexities of international education, providing tailored advice and support to achieve their academic and career goals.

For further inquiries or consultation, you can reach Kirtish at kirtishdatwani1@gmail.com or contact his team directly at 9998294089. Kirtish Datwani is based in India.